ABBA
FOR CLASSICAL PIANO

CONTENTS

Cover photo courtesy: Pictorial Press/Cache Agency

— PIANO LEVEL —
LATE INTERMEDIATE/EARLY ADVANCED

ISBN 978-1-4950-5908-7

HAL•LEONARD®
CORPORATION

7777 W. BLUEMOUND RD. P.O. BOX 13819 MILWAUKEE, WI 53213

Visit Hal Leonard Online at
www.halleonard.com

Visit Phillip at
www.phillipkeveren.com

PREFACE

The statistics are staggering. To say ABBA is one of the most successful pop groups in history hardly seems extravagant enough.

- Their compilation CD *ABBA Gold*, released in 1992, has sold more than 28 million copies to date.

- 1999 saw the London premiere of the hugely successful musical *Mamma Mia!*, based on the songs of ABBA. The musical opened on Broadway two years later, and today it is the world's most popular show, having been seen by more than 42 million people.

- As I write this preface, a YouTube posting of "Dancing Queen" has been viewed 101,493,687 times. Gulp!

The Swedish pop quartet first saw success in the 1970s with a string of worldwide hits. With keyboards playing a prominent role in many of these recordings, their songs are a delight to arrange for solo piano.

Various styles of classical literature inspire all of these settings. "The Winner Takes It All" and "Fernando" mine the Romantic style of classical piano literature, while "Chiquita" uses a Bach two-part invention as a springboard.

I hope you enjoy playing these arrangements!

Sincerely,

Phillip Keveren

BIOGRAPHY

Phillip Keveren, a multi-talented keyboard artist and composer, has composed original works in a variety of genres from piano solo to symphonic orchestra. Mr. Keveren gives frequent concerts and workshops for teachers and their students in the United States, Canada, Europe, and Asia. Mr. Keveren holds a B.M. in composition from California State University Northridge and a M.M. in composition from the University of Southern California.

CHIQUITITA
(incorporating J.S. Bach's Two-Part Invention No. 14)

Words and Music by BENNY ANDERSSON
and BJÖRN ULVAEUS
Arranged by Phillip Keveren

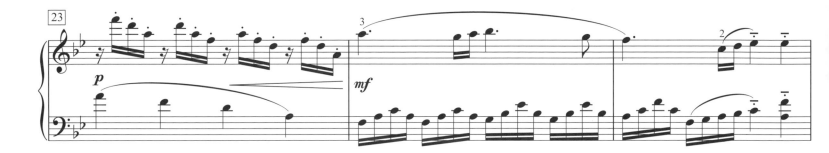

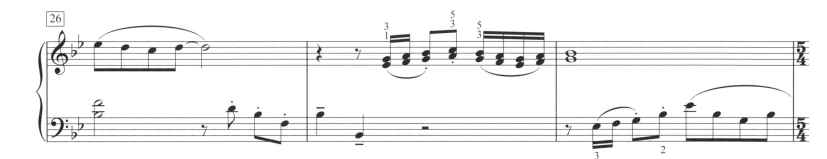

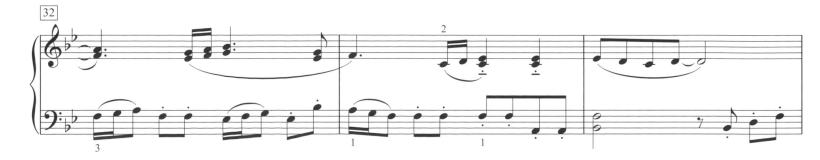

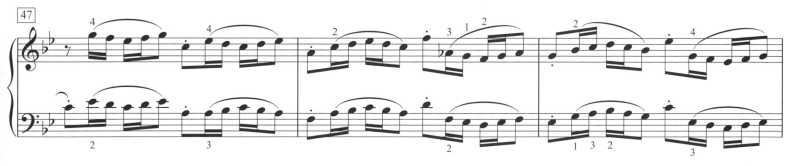

DANCING QUEEN

Words and Music by BENNY ANDERSSON,
BJÖRN ULVAEUS and STIG ANDERSON
Arranged by Phillip Keveren

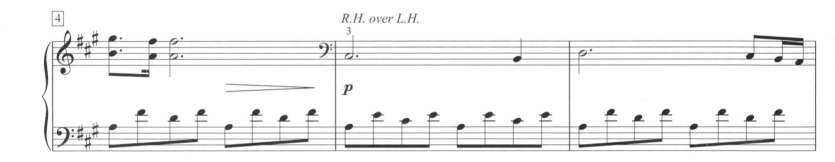

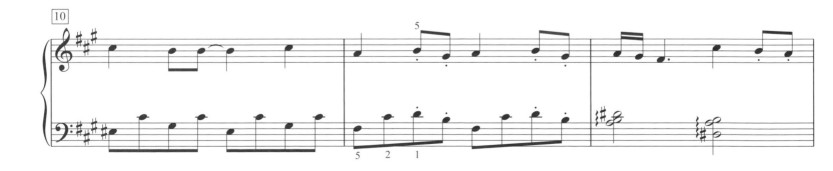

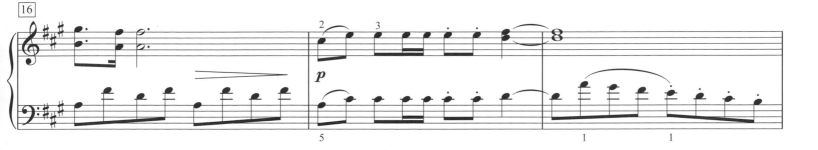

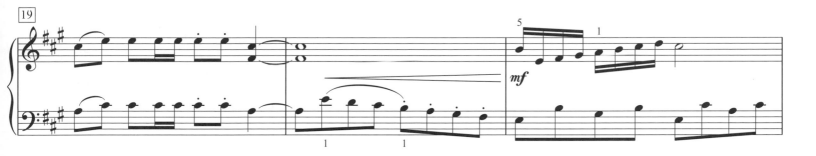

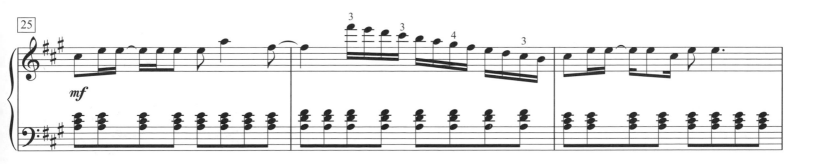

FERNANDO

Words and Music by BENNY ANDERSSON,
BJÖRN ULVAEUS and STIG ANDERSON
Arranged by Phillip Keveren

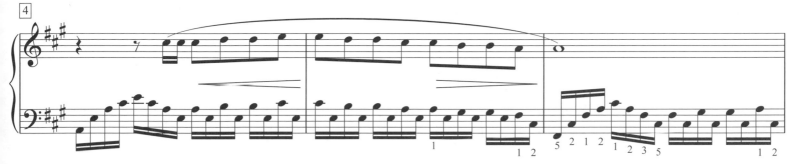

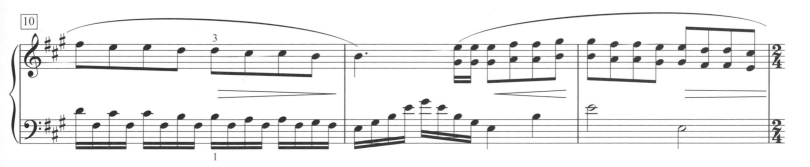

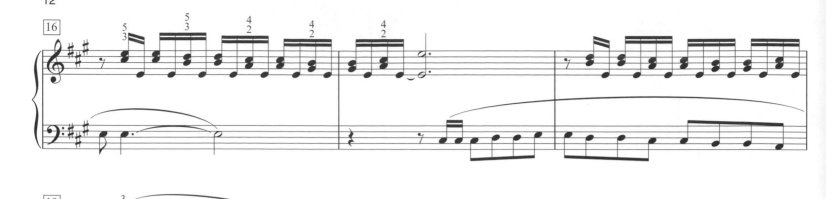

DOES YOUR MOTHER KNOW

Words and Music by BENNY ANDERSSON
and BJÖRN ULVAEUS
Arranged by Phillip Keveren

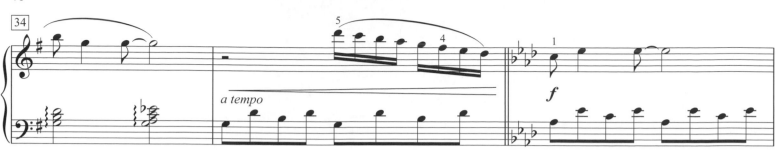

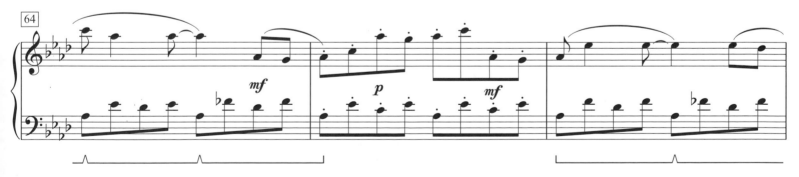

GIMME! GIMME! GIMME!
(A Man After Midnight)

Words and Music by BENNY ANDERSSON
and BJÖRN ULVAEUS
Arranged by Phillip Keveren

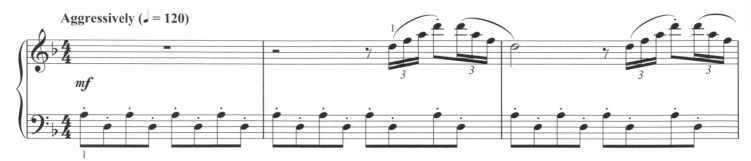

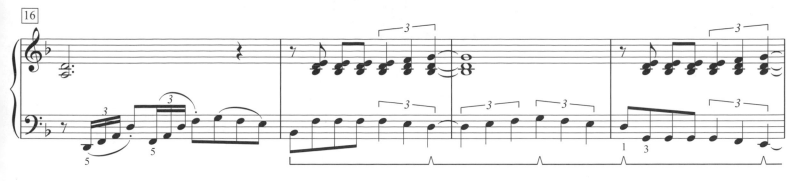

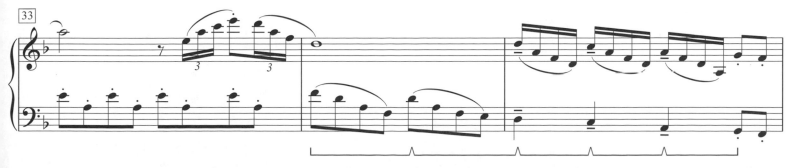

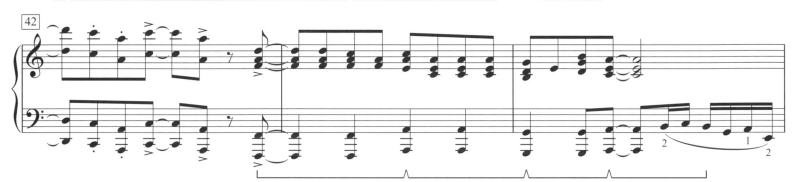

S.O.S.

Words and Music by BENNY ANDERSSON,
BJÖRN ULVAEUS and STIG ANDERSON
Arranged by Phillip Keveren

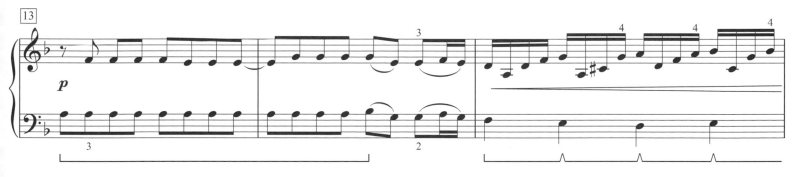

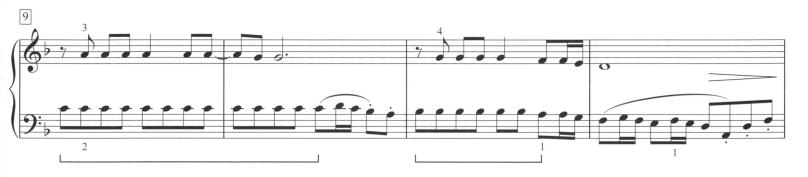

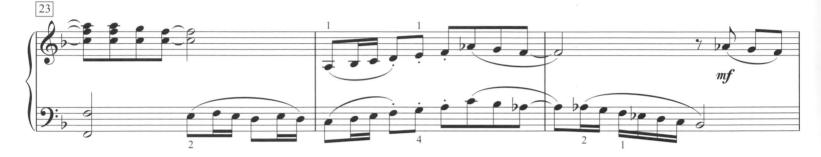

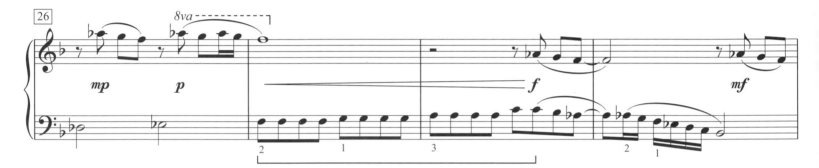

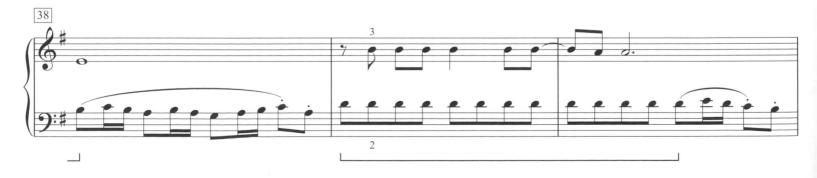

I HAVE A DREAM

Words and Music by BENNY ANDERSSON
and BJÖRN ULVAEUS
Arranged by Phillip Keveren

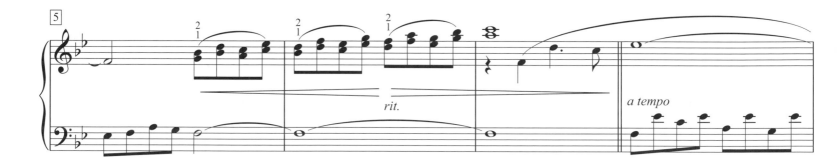

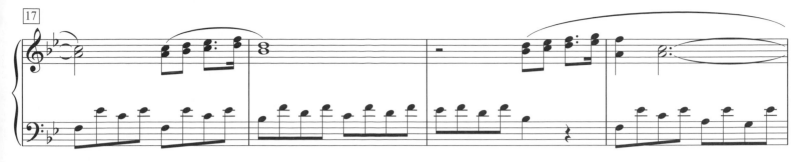

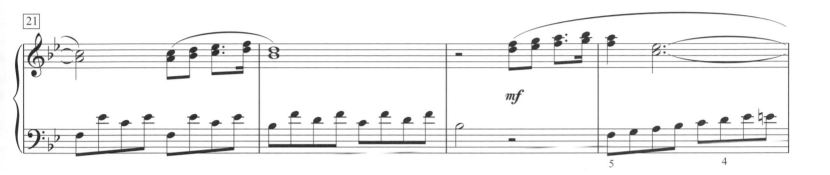

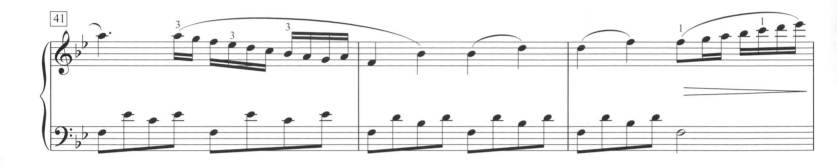

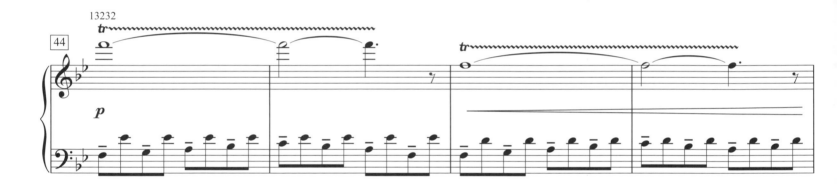

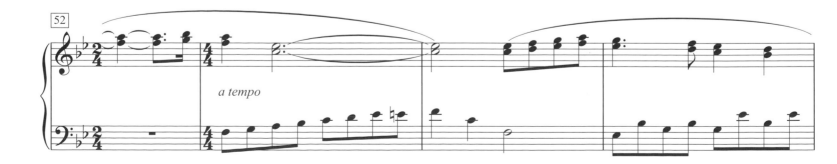

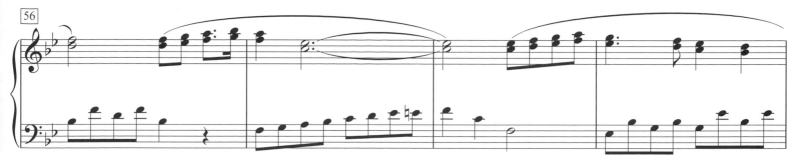

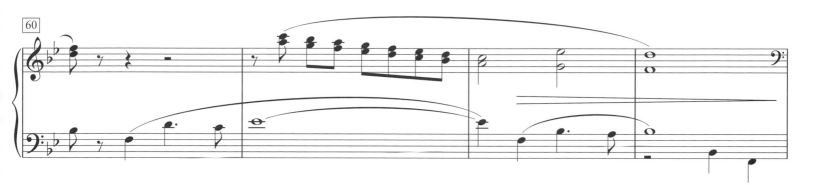

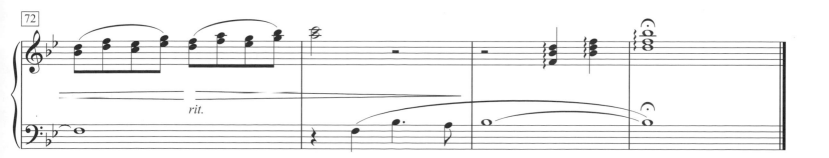

KNOWING ME, KNOWING YOU

Words and Music by BENNY ANDERSSON,
BJÖRN ULVAEUS and STIG ANDERSON
Arranged by Phillip Keveren

Dreamily, with rubato (♩ = 96–100)

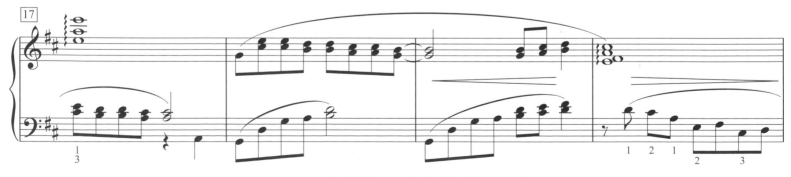

MAMMA MIA

Words and Music by BENNY ANDERSSON,
BJÖRN ULVAEUS and STIG ANDERSON
Arranged by Phillip Keveren

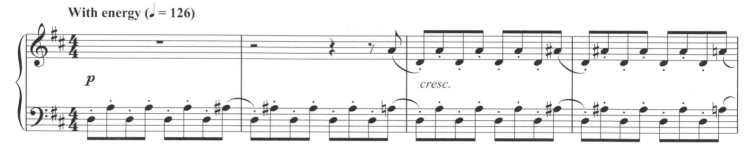

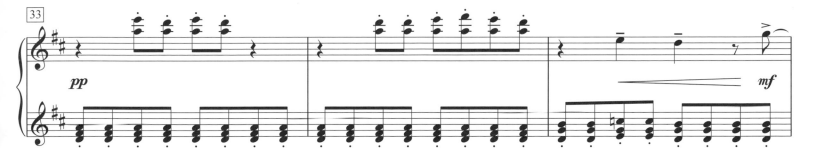

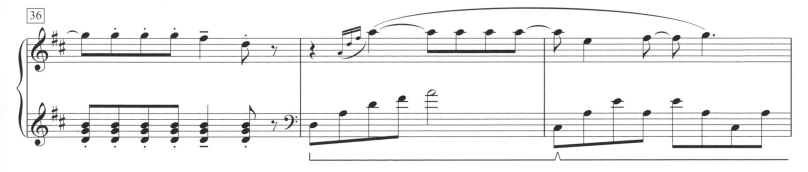

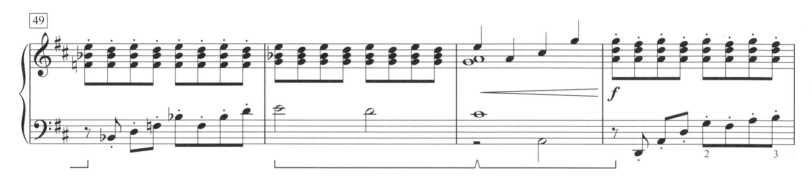

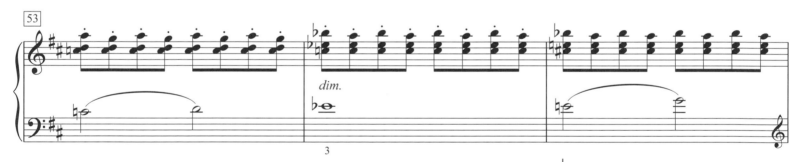

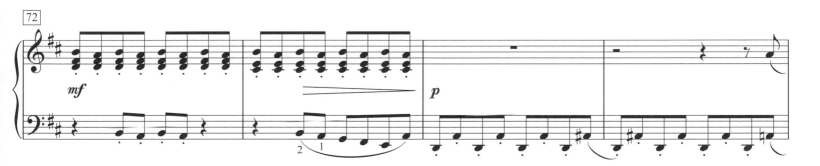

MONEY, MONEY, MONEY
(incorporating Beethoven's "Für Elise")

Words and Music by BENNY ANDERSSON
and BJÖRN ULVAEUS
Arranged by Phillip Keveren

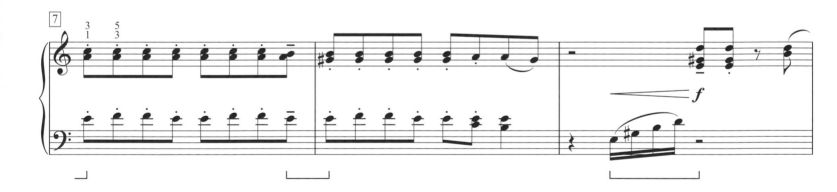

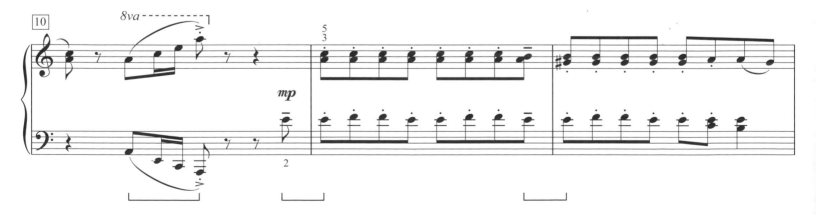

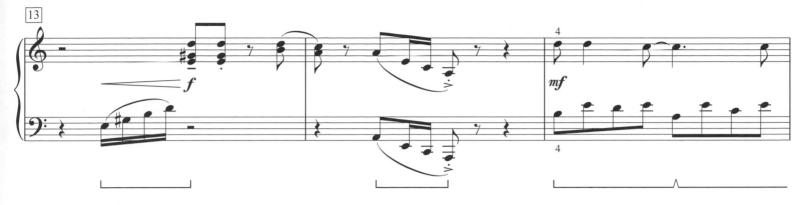

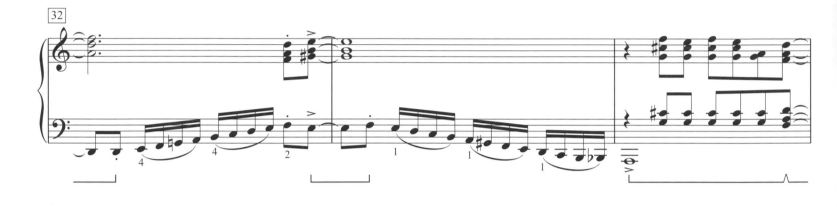

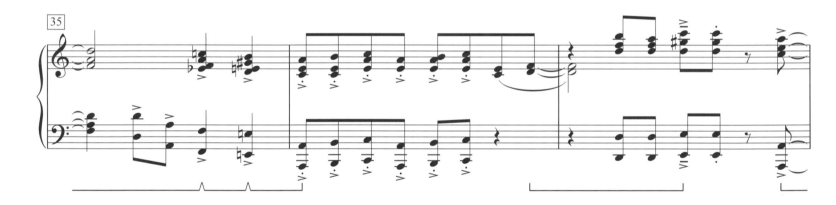

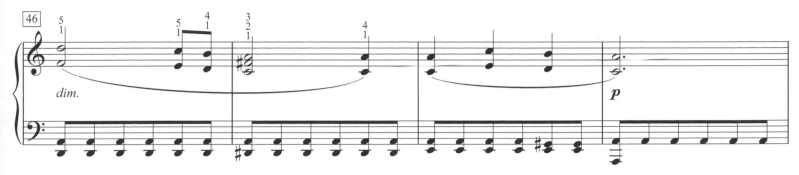

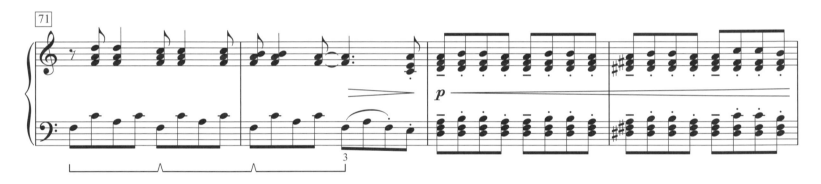

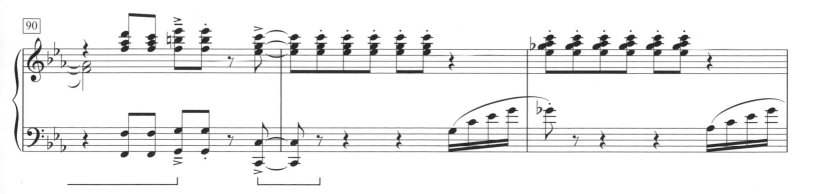

SUPER TROUPER

Words and Music by BENNY ANDERSSON
and BJÖRN ULVAEUS
Arranged by Phillip Keveren

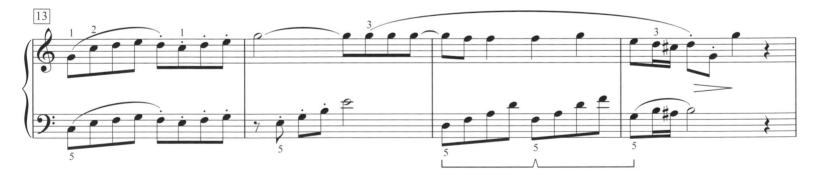

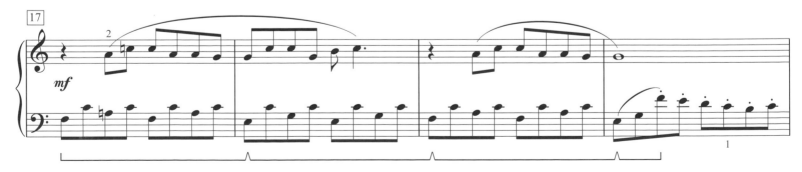

41

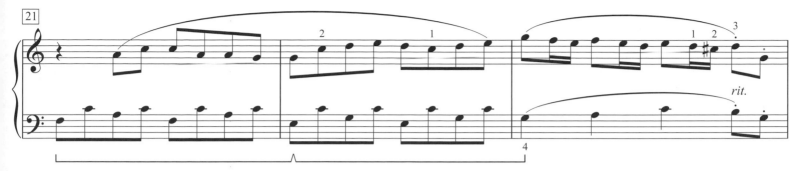

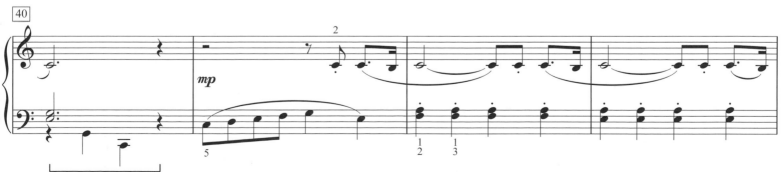

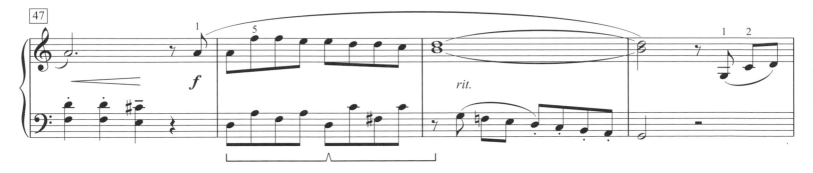

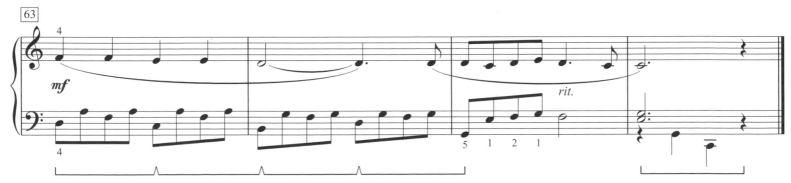

TAKE A CHANCE ON ME

Words and Music by BENNY ANDERSSON
and BJÖRN ULVAEUS
Arranged by Phillip Keveren

WATERLOO

Words and Music by BENNY ANDERSSON,
BJÖRN ULVAEUS and STIG ANDERSON
Arranged by Phillip Keveren

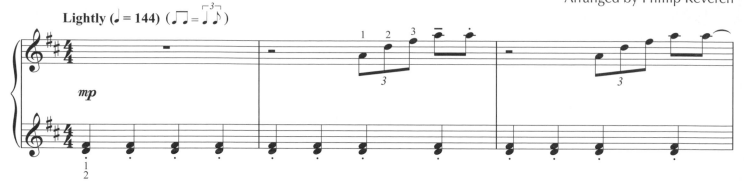

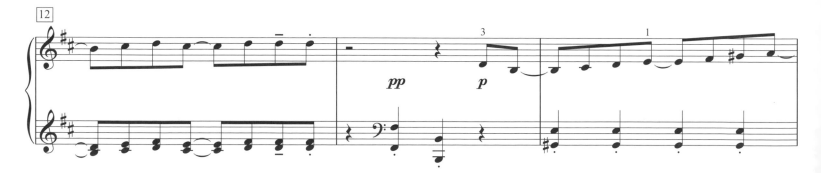

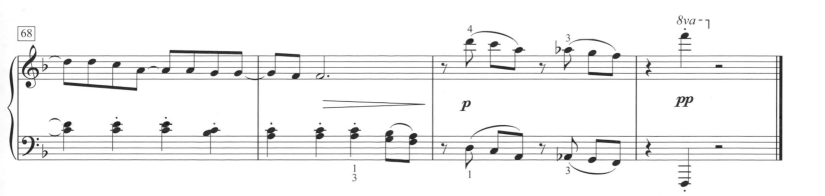

THE WINNER TAKES IT ALL

Words and Music by BENNY ANDERSSON
and BJÖRN ULVAEUS
Arranged by Phillip Keveren

Passionately, with freedom (♩ = 108–112)

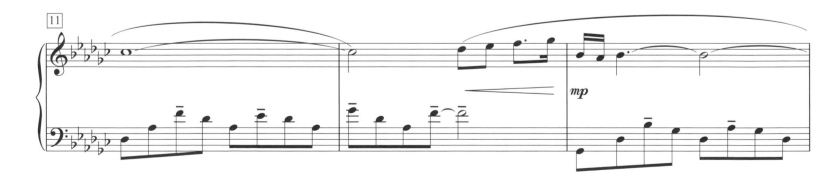

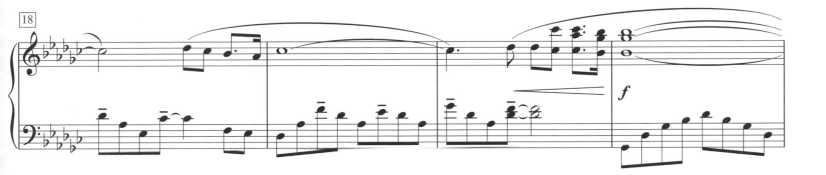

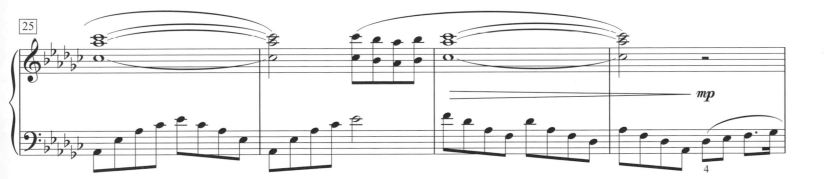

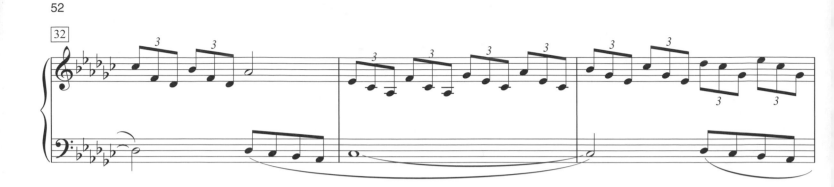

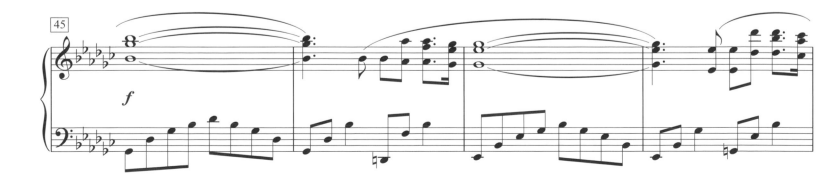

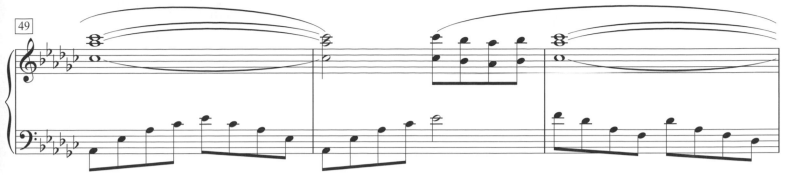

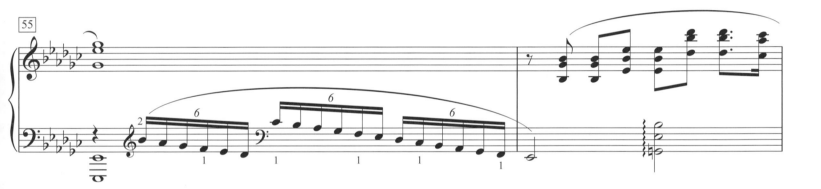

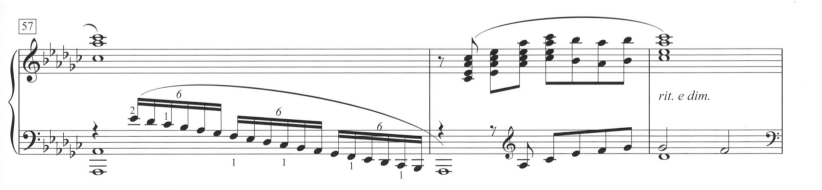

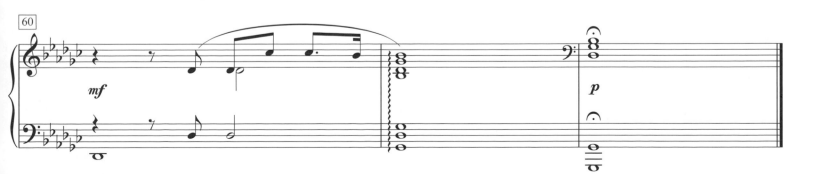

THANK YOU FOR THE MUSIC

Words and Music by BENNY ANDERSSON
and BJÖRN ULVAEUS
Arranged by Phillip Keveren

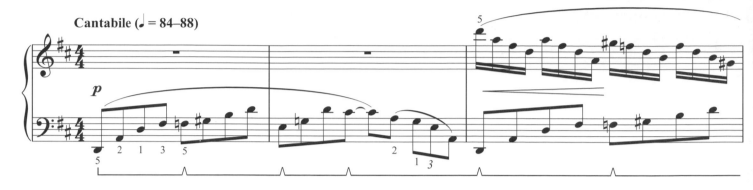